T0400921

FORCES IN MOTION

SPINNING AND ROLLING

by Spencer Brinker

Consultant: Beth Gambro
Reading Specialist, Yorkville, Illinois

BEARPORT
PUBLISHING

Minneapolis, Minnesota

Teaching Tips

Before Reading

- Look at the cover of the book. Discuss the picture and the title.
- Ask readers to brainstorm a list of what they already know about spinning and rolling. What can they expect to see in this book?
- Go on a picture walk, looking through the pictures to discuss vocabulary and make predictions about the text.

During Reading

- Read for purpose. Encourage readers to think about when things spin and roll in their own lives as they are reading.
- Ask readers to look for the details of the book. What are they learning about spinning and rolling? What is the difference?
- If readers encounter an unknown word, ask them to look at the sounds in the word. Then, ask them to look at the rest of the page. Are there any clues to help them understand?

After Reading

- Encourage readers to pick a buddy and reread the book together.
- Ask readers to name one thing from the book that spins and one that rolls. Go back and find the pages that tell about these things.
- Ask readers to write or draw something they learned about spinning and rolling.

Credits: Cover and title page, © FSB Professional/Shutterstock, © Augenstern/Shutterstock; 3, © NickyBlade/iStock, © PHILIPIMAGE/Shutterstock; 4, © Morten Watkins/Shutterstock; 5, © Werner Stoffberg/Shutterstock; 6, © valio84sl/iStock, © roundex/Shutterstock; 7, © JuiceBros/iStock; 8,9, © fazon1/iStock, © malerapaso/iStock; 10,11, © Utamaru Kido/Getty, © baona/iStock, © rubanlena/Shutterstock; 12,13, © FatCamera/iStock; 14,15, © Cultura RM /Alamy; 16,17, © GGKEAX/Alamy; 18,19, © Paul Biris/Getty; 20, © bolton09/iStock; 21, © Lynda Disher/Shutterstock; 22L, © imtmphoto/iStock; 22R, © Georgii Shipin/Shutterstock, © Lightspring/Shutterstock; 23TL, © fokke baarssen/Shutterstock; 23TR, © Dome Studio/iStock; 23BL, © Juanmonino/iStock; 23BR, © kali9/iStock.

Library of Congress Cataloging-in-Publication Data is available at www.loc.gov or upon request from the publisher.

ISBN: 978-1-63691-412-1 (hardcover)
ISBN: 978-1-63691-417-6 (paperback)
ISBN: 978-1-63691-422-0 (ebook)

For more information, write to Bearport Publishing, 5357 Penn Avenue South, Minneapolis, MN 55419. Printed in the United States of America.

Contents

Around and Around

Look at that top.

It spins fast!

See the ball roll.

It goes down the hill.

Spinning and rolling are two ways things can move.

What spins?

A fan spins.

So does a merry-go-round.

They move in circles.

6

When things spin, they turn.

But they do not change places.

Their middles stay in the same spot.

Middle

9

Sometimes, things move to new places when they turn.

This is rolling.

A pencil rolls on a desk.

It turns around its **center** and changes places.

Rolling can help us move things.

Wheels roll when they turn.

The wheels of a bike take us to new places.

Whee!

13

A wagon has wheels, too.

When you pull it, the wheels roll.

14

Pulling is a **force**.

A force can make something move.

15

Things need force to spin, too.

The force of air pushes the **blades** of a windmill.

They spin around and around.

Blade

Some things need lots of force to move.

This snowball is big!

I need to push hard to roll it.

It takes a lot of **energy**.

Forces move things all around us.

Many of them go in a circle.

You can spin or roll, too!

Sometimes Spins and Sometimes Rolls

A basketball can both spin and roll. Let's take a look!

Some people can spin a basketball on their finger. The ball turns in the same place!

On the ground, turning moves the ball. It rolls away.

22

Glossary

blades flat parts of a windmill that spin around a center

center the middle point or part of something

energy a measure of how much work something can do

force a push or pull that makes things move

Index

Read More

Enz, Tammy. *Discover Forces (Discover Physical Science)*. North Mankato, MN: Pebble, 2020.

Enz, Tammy. *Discover Motion (Discover Physical Science)*. North Mankato, MN: Pebble, 2021.

Learn More Online

1. Go to **www.factsurfer.com** or scan the QR code below.
2. Enter "**Spinning and Rolling**" into the search box.
3. Click on the cover of this book to see a list of websites.

About the Author

Spencer Brinker lives in Minnesota with his family. Their dog, Linzer, rolls in the grass and spins around before lying down.